Grandma's Recipe Treats

Packed with Tasty & Traditional Dishes

**FLAME TREE
PUBLISHING**

Contents

Introduction ∞

G randma is a very special person who sits at the heart of the family. She should be celebrated because no one could ever bake bread, knit a scarf, grow vegetables or tell a story like she can.

One of our favourite things about Grandma is that she knows how to cook! The aroma of those hearty stews and home-baked bread as you step into Grandma's house imprint themselves as lasting fond memories from childhood. Going to visit Grandma has long been twinned with the excitement of knowing she will pluck out some goodies from her cupboard, made by her own fair hands. Somehow she knows just how to make the perfect treats which become firm family favourites, whether it is a warm broth to greet you inside from the cold or a delicious cake to indulge in.

Grandma also knows her way around the home and kitchen, providing a wealth of wisdom. She knows that a routine is the best way to keep a house and garden shipshape; that vinegar and newspaper is the best thing for cleaning windows and mirrors; that bicarbonate of soda banishes smells from larders and fridges; that lemon juice cleans brass and copper and 'bleaches' wooden chopping boards clean. She is even full of little gems such as how to turn a dish towel into an apron or how to use common kitchen items to make a face mask.

This delightful book celebrates the wit and wisdom Grandma provides, with a wide selection of traditional recipes, just like Grandma used to make. It is also packed with homely hints and tips and wise grandmotherly advice, poems and household craft ideas.

Rustic Country Bread ∽

Makes 1 large loaf

Ingredients

For the sourdough starter:
225 g/8 oz/2 cups strong white/bread flour
2 tsp easy-blend dried yeast
300 ml/½ pint/1¼ cups warm water

For the bread dough:
350 g/12 oz/3 cups strong white/bread flour
3 tbsp rye flour
1½ tsp salt
½ tsp caster/superfine sugar
1 tsp dried yeast
1 tsp sunflower/corn oil
175 ml/6 fl oz/scant ¾ cup warm water

To finish:
2 tsp plain/all-purpose flour; 2 tsp rye flour

Preheat the oven to 220°C/425°F/Gas Mark 7, 15 minutes before baking. For the starter, sift the flour into a bowl. Stir in the yeast and make a well in the centre. Pour in the warm water and mix with a fork. Transfer to a saucepan, cover with a clean dish towel and leave for 2–3 days at room temperature. Stir the mixture and spray with a little water twice a day.

For the dough, mix the dry ingredients in a bowl. Add 250 ml/8 fl oz/1 cup of the starter, the oil and the warm water. Mix to a soft dough. Knead on a lightly floured surface for 10 minutes until smooth and elastic. Put in an oiled bowl, cover and leave to rise in a warm place for about 1½ hours until doubled in size.

Turn the dough out and knead for a minute or two. Shape into a round loaf. Place on an oiled baking sheet. Cover with oiled plastic wrap and leave to rise for 1 hour, or until doubled in size.

Dust the loaf with flour. With a sharp knife, make slashes across the top. Slash across the loaf in the opposite direction to make a grid pattern. Bake in the oven for 40–45 minutes until golden brown and hollow-sounding when tapped underneath. Cool on a wire rack and serve.

Grandma's Recipes

This has always puzzled me, just how much is a pinch?
These recipes of dear Grandma's surely are no cinch.
A 'snip' of this, a 'dab' of that, a 'lump' of something else,
Then 'beat it for a little while', or, 'stir until it melts.'
I have to be a wizard to decipher what she meant,
By all these strange proportions in her cookbook worn and bent.
How much nutmeg in the doughnuts? Grandma wouldn't flinch,
As she said, with twinkling eyes, 'Oh, just about a pinch.'
There must have been in her wise head a measuring device,
That told her just how much to use of sugar, salt and spice.

Author Unknown

Cheese-Crusted Potato Scones ∽

Serves 4

Ingredients

200 g/7 oz/1¾ cups self-raising flour
3 tbsp wholemeal/whole-wheat flour
½ tsp salt
1½ tsp baking powder
25 g/1 oz/2 tbsp butter, cubed
5 tbsp milk
175 g/6 oz/¼ cup cold mashed potato
freshly ground black pepper
2 tbsp milk
40 g/1½ oz/6 tbsp finely grated mature Cheddar cheese
paprika, to dust
basil sprig, to garnish

Preheat the oven to 220°C/425°F/Gas Mark 7, 15 minutes before baking. Sift the flours, salt and baking powder into a large bowl. Rub in the butter until the mixture resembles fine breadcrumbs. Stir 4 tablespoons of the milk into the mashed potato and season with black pepper. Add the dry ingredients to the potato mixture, mixing together with a fork and adding the remaining 1 tablespoon of milk if needed.

Knead the dough on a lightly floured surface for a few seconds until smooth. Roll out to a 15 cm/6 inch round and transfer to an oiled baking sheet.

Mark the scone round into six wedges, cutting about halfway through with a small sharp knife. Brush with milk, then sprinkle with the cheese and a faint dusting of paprika.

Bake on the middle shelf of the preheated oven for 15 minutes, or until well risen and golden brown. Transfer to a wire rack and leave to cool for 5 minutes before breaking into wedges.

Serve warm or leave to cool completely. Once cool, store the scones in an airtight tin. Garnish with a basil sprig and serve split and buttered.

Grandma's Tip

Rub olive oil over your hands before kneading dough – it will stop the mixture sticking to your hands.

Kitchen Cleaning Tips

Clean copper pans by cutting a fresh lemon in half and dipping it in baking powder. Use it to rub the surface of the pan. Wipe clean with fresh water and dry carefully.

Preparing soft fruits? Washing surfaces, bowls and hands with white vinegar and rinsing well with water afterwards will remove any stains.

Rinse dishcloths and washing-up sponges after use in a solution of hot water and bicarbonate of soda/baking soda to keep them smelling like roses.

This makes a little apron that ties around your waist. Take a large tea towel/dish towel and 2 metres/3 yards of ribbon – you could buy both of these from your local market. Fold your towel in half lengthways with the pattern facing inwards.

Take your ribbon and place it along the length of the fold of the towel. Align the middle of the ribbon with the middle of the towel edge, so that there are equal lengths of ribbon on either side, and pin it to keep it in place.

Sew the ribbon through both layers of the towel, stitching all the way along each edge of the ribbon, so that it is firmly fixed. Fold the top towel layer towards the ribbon, placing the edge of the towel directly below the ribbon – this will become the pocket.

Sew along the side edges of the pocket, sewing through just the pocket layers. Make sure the thread is secure and will hold when something is placed in the pocket. If you wish to, you can also sew down the middle of the pocket, effectively giving yourself two smaller pockets.

Admire your creation and try it on by using the ribbon to tie the apron around your waist.

Multigrain Bread

Makes 1 large loaf

Ingredients
350 g/12 oz/3 cups strong white/bread flour
2 tsp salt
225 g/8 oz/2 cups granary flour/granary
   bread flour or whole-wheat bread flour
125 g/4 oz/1 cup rye flour
25 g/1 oz/2 tbsp butter, diced
2 tsp easy-blend dried yeast
25 g/1 oz/⅓ cup rolled oats
2 tbsp sunflower seeds
1 tbsp malt extract
450 ml/¾ pint/2 cups warm water
1 egg, beaten

Preheat the oven to 220°C/425°F/Gas Mark 7, 15 minutes before baking. Sift the white flour and salt into a large bowl. Stir in the granary and rye flours, then rub in the butter until the mixture resembles breadcrumbs. Stir in the yeast, oats and seeds and make a well in the centre.

Stir the malt extract into the warm water until dissolved. Add the malt water to the dry ingredients. Mix to a soft dough. Turn the dough out onto a lightly floured surface and knead for 10 minutes until smooth and elastic.

Put in an oiled bowl, cover with plastic wrap and leave to rise in a warm place for 1½ hours, or until doubled in size. Turn out and knead again for a minute or two to knock out the air. Shape into an oval loaf about 30.5 cm/12 inches long and place on a well-oiled baking sheet. Cover with oiled plastic wrap and leave to rise for 40 minutes, or until doubled in size.

Brush the loaf with beaten egg and bake in the preheated oven for 35–45 minutes until the bread is well risen, browned and sounds hollow when the base is tapped. Leave to cool on a wire rack, then serve.

Rosemary & Olive Focaccia

Makes 2 loaves

Ingredients

700 g/1½ lb/5½ cups strong white/bread flour
pinch salt
pinch caster/superfine sugar
7 g/¼ oz sachet easy-blend dried/active dry yeast
2 tsp freshly chopped rosemary
450 ml/¾ pint/1¾ cups warm water
3 tbsp olive oil
75 g/3 oz/½ cup pitted black/ripe olives,
   roughly chopped
rosemary sprigs, to garnish

To finish:
3 tbsp olive oil
coarse sea salt
freshly ground black pepper

Preheat the oven to 200°C/400°F/Gas Mark 6, 15 minutes before baking. Sift the flour, salt and sugar into a large bowl. Stir in the yeast and rosemary. Make a well in the centre.

Pour in the warm water and the oil and mix to a soft dough. Turn out onto a lightly floured surface and knead for about 10 minutes until smooth and elastic.

Pat the olives dry on absorbent paper towels, then gently knead into the dough. Put in an oiled bowl, cover with plastic wrap and leave to rise in a warm place for 1½ hours, or until it has doubled in size.

Turn out the dough and knead again for a minute or two. Divide in half and roll out each piece to a 25.5 cm/10 inch circle. Transfer to oiled baking sheets, cover with oiled plastic wrap and leave to rise for 30 minutes.

Using the fingertips, make deep dimples all over the dough. Drizzle with the oil and sprinkle with sea salt. Bake in the preheated oven for 20–25 minutes until risen and golden. Cool on a wire rack and garnish with sprigs of rosemary. Grind over a little black pepper before serving.

Natural Remedies

You might be surprised to discover how common items found in
your kitchen can be used to cure and ease all sorts of problems.

Lemon

Lemon is a great way to help relieve flu and cold symptoms.
Drinking fresh lemon juice or lemon in hot
water is also a great way to cleanse the system.

Onion

Use raw slices (or a homemade lotion of onion juice and salt) directly
on the skin for natural relief from burns, insect bites and stings.
Use a poultice of roasted onion for earache.

Cucumber

Place a cucumber slice over strained or inflamed eyes.
Apply fresh cucumber or cucumber juice to sunburn to cool.

Bread

Apply fresh bread to shallow wounds
to help stop the bleeding.
Apply a warm bread poultice to
infected cuts to reduce itching and pain.

Bacon, Mushroom & Cheese Puffs ⌒

Makes 8

Ingredients

1 tbsp olive oil
225 g/8 oz/2½ cups wiped and
    roughly chopped field mushrooms
225 g/8 oz/½ lb rindless streaky
    bacon, roughly chopped
2 tbsp freshly chopped parsley
salt and freshly ground black pepper
350 g/12 oz/¾ lb ready-rolled puff
    pastry dough sheet, thawed if frozen
25 g/1 oz/¼ cup grated Emmenthal/
    Swiss cheese
1 egg, beaten
rocket/arugula or watercress,
    to garnish
tomatoes, to serve

Preheat the oven to 200°C/400°F/Gas Mark 6, 15 minutes before baking. Heat the olive oil in a large frying pan. Add the mushrooms and bacon and fry for 6–8 minutes until golden in colour. Stir in the parsley, season to taste with salt and pepper and allow to cool.

Roll the sheet of pastry dough a little thinner on a lightly floured surface until you have a 30.5 cm/12 inch square. Cut the dough into four equal squares.

Stir the grated cheese into the mushroom mixture. Spoon a quarter of the mixture onto one half of each square. Brush the edges of each square with a little of the beaten egg. Fold over the dough to form triangular parcels. Seal the edges well and place on a lightly oiled baking sheet. Make shallow slashes in the tops of the parcels with a knife and brush with the remaining beaten egg. Cook in the preheated oven for 20 minutes, or until puffy and golden brown. Serve warm or cold, garnished with the rocket/arugula or watercress and served with tomatoes.

Tomato & Basil Soup

Serves 4

Ingredients

7 ripe tomatoes, cut in half
2 garlic cloves, unpeeled
1 tsp olive oil
1 tbsp balsamic vinegar
1 tbsp dark brown sugar
1 tbsp tomato purée/paste
300 ml/½ pint/1¼ cups vegetable stock
6 tbsp low-fat natural/plain yogurt
2 tbsp freshly chopped basil
salt and freshly ground black pepper
small basil leaves, to garnish

Preheat the oven to 200°C/400°F/Gas Mark 6. Evenly spread the tomatoes and garlic in a single layer in a large roasting tin/pan.

Mix the oil and vinegar together. Drizzle over the tomatoes and sprinkle with the dark brown sugar. Roast the tomatoes in the preheated oven for 20 minutes until tender and lightly charred in places. Remove from the oven and allow to cool slightly. When cool enough to handle, squeeze the softened flesh of the garlic from the papery skins. Place with the charred tomatoes in a nylon sieve over a saucepan.

Press the garlic and tomato through the sieve with the back of a wooden spoon. When all the flesh has been sieved, add the tomato purée/paste and vegetable stock to the pan. Heat gently, stirring occasionally.

In a small bowl, beat the yogurt and basil together and season to taste with salt and pepper. Stir the basil yogurt into the soup. Garnish with basil leaves and serve immediately.

Beautiful Old Age

It ought to be lovely to be old
to be full of the peace that comes of experience
and wrinkled ripe fulfilment.

The wrinkled smile of completeness that follows a life
lived undaunted and unsoured with accepted lies
they would ripen like apples, and be scented like pippins
in their old age.

Soothing, old people should be, like apples
when one is tired of love.
Fragrant like yellowing leaves, and dim with the soft
stillness and satisfaction of autumn.

And a girl should say:
It must be wonderful to live and grow old.
Look at my mother, how rich and still she is!

And a young man should think: By Jove
my father has faced all weathers, but it's been a life!

by D.H. Lawrence (1885–1930)

Carrot & Ginger Soup ∽

Serves 4

Ingredients

4 slices bread, crusts removed
1 tsp yeast extract
2 tsp olive oil
1 onion, peeled and chopped
1 garlic clove, peeled and crushed
½ tsp ground ginger
7 large carrots, peeled and chopped
1 litre/1¾ pints/4 cups vegetable stock
2.5 cm/1 inch piece root ginger, peeled
    and finely grated
salt and freshly ground black pepper
1 tbsp lemon juice

To garnish:
chives
lemon zest

Preheat the oven to 180°C/350°F/Gas Mark 4. Roughly chop the bread. Dissolve the yeast extract in 2 tablespoons warm water and mix with the bread.

Spread the bread cubes over a lightly oiled baking sheet and bake for 20 minutes, turning halfway through. Remove from the oven and reserve.

Heat the oil in a large saucepan. Gently cook the onion and garlic for 3–4 minutes. Stir in the ground ginger and cook for 1 minute to release the flavour. Add the chopped carrots, then stir in the stock and the fresh ginger. Simmer gently for 15 minutes.

Remove from the heat and allow to cool a little. Blend until smooth, then season to taste with salt and pepper. Stir in the lemon juice. Garnish with the chives and lemon zest and serve immediately with the garlic croutons.

Italian Meatballs in Tomato Sauce

Serves 4

Ingredients

For the tomato sauce:
4 tbsp olive oil
1 large onion, peeled and finely chopped
2 garlic cloves, peeled and chopped
400 g/14 oz canned chopped tomatoes
1 tbsp sun-dried tomato paste
1 tbsp dried mixed herbs
150 ml/¼ pint/⅔ cup water
salt and freshly ground black pepper

For the meatballs:
450 g/1 lb fresh minced/ground pork
50 g/2 oz/1 cup fresh breadcrumbs
1 egg yolk
75 g/3 oz/¾ cup grated Parmesan cheese
20 small stuffed green olives

freshly snipped chives, to garnish
freshly cooked pasta, to serve

To make the tomato sauce, heat half the olive oil in a saucepan and cook half the chopped onion for 5 minutes until softened. Add the garlic, chopped tomatoes, sun-dried tomato paste, mixed herbs and water to the pan and season to taste with salt and pepper. Stir well until blended. Bring to the boil, then cover and simmer for 15 minutes.

To make the meatballs, place the pork, breadcrumbs, remaining onion, egg yolk and half the Parmesan in a large bowl. Season well and mix together with your hands. Divide the mixture into 20 balls.

Flatten one ball out in the palms of your hands, place an olive in the centre, then squeeze the meat around the olive to enclose completely. Repeat with the remaining mixture and olives. Place the meatballs on a baking sheet, cover with plastic wrap and chill in the refrigerator for 30 minutes.

Heat the remaining oil in a large frying pan and cook the meatballs for 8–10 minutes, turning occasionally, until golden brown. Pour in the sauce and heat through. Sprinkle with chives and the remaining Parmesan. Serve immediately with the freshly cooked pasta.

Household Wisdom: Dinner Parties ∽

It is lovely to welcome friends, neighbours and relatives into our homes, and here are some tips to keep in mind when entertaining. The only danger in being a good host or hostess is getting guests to go home again!

If you have invited friends round to dinner, plan what you will be serving well in advance.

Pools of light from small lamps dotted around a room make it look cosier than a single bright ceiling light.

Candles will burn for longer if they are cold: put your candles in the fridge before a dinner party.

Flowers make a lovely decoration. When buying flowers, buy those which are still in bud, as they will be the youngest in the shop and will last longer.

Slow Roasted Lamb

Serves 6

Ingredients

1 leg of lamb, about 1.5 kg/3 lb in weight
2 tbsp vegetable oil
1 tsp fennel seeds
1 tsp cumin seeds
1 tsp ground coriander
1 tsp turmeric
2 garlic cloves, peeled and crushed
2 green chillies, deseeded and chopped
freshly cooked vegetables, to serve

For the potatoes:
550 g/1 lb 3 oz potatoes, peeled
2 onions, peeled
4 garlic cloves, peeled

Preheat the oven to 190°C/375°F/Gas Mark 5. Wipe the lamb with absorbent paper towels and make small slits over the lamb. Reserve.

Heat the oil in a frying pan, add the seeds and fry for 30 seconds, stirring. Add the remaining spices including the 2 garlic cloves and green chillies and cook for 5 minutes. Remove and use half to spread over the lamb.

Cut the potatoes into bite-size chunks and the onions into wedges. Cut the garlic in half. Place in a roasting tin and cover with the remaining spice paste, then place the lamb on top.

Cook in the preheated oven for 1¼–1½ hours until the lamb and potatoes are cooked. Turn the potatoes over occasionally during cooking. Serve the lamb with the potatoes and freshly cooked vegetables..

Pan-Fried Beef with Creamy Mushrooms ∽

Serves 4

Ingredients

225 g/8 oz shallots (about 10), peeled
2 garlic cloves, peeled
2 tbsp olive oil
4 medallions of beef
4 plum tomatoes, rinsed and cut into eighths
125 g/4 oz/1¾ cups wiped and sliced
    flat mushrooms
3 tbsp brandy
150 ml/¼ pint/⅔ cup red wine
salt and freshly ground black pepper
4 tbsp double/heavy cream

To serve:
baby new potatoes
freshly cooked green beans

Cut the shallots in half if large, then chop the garlic. Heat the oil in a large frying pan and cook the shallots for about 8 minutes, stirring occasionally, until almost softened. Add the garlic and beef and cook for 8–10 minutes, turning once during cooking, until the meat is browned all over. Using a slotted spoon, transfer the beef to a plate and keep warm.

Add the tomatoes and mushrooms to the pan and cook for 5 minutes, stirring frequently, until the mushrooms have softened.

Pour in the brandy and heat through. Draw the pan off the heat and carefully ignite. Allow the flames to subside. Pour in the wine, return to the heat and bring to the boil. Boil until reduced by one third. Draw the pan off the heat, season to taste with salt and pepper, add the cream and stir.

Arrange the beef on serving plates and spoon over the sauce. Serve with baby new potatoes and a few green beans.

Grandma's Tip

If you've just been chopping onions or garlic, peeling potatoes or handling fish, sprinkle some bicarbonate of soda/baking soda onto wet hands, and then rinse off. The smell will be gone!

Grace

For what we are about to receive,
May the Lord make us truly thankful.

Traditional, Author Unknown

Lancashire Hotpot

Serves 4

Ingredients

1 kg/2¼ lb middle end neck of lamb,
    divided into cutlets
2 tbsp vegetable oil
2 large onions, peeled and sliced
2 tsp plain/all-purpose flour
150 ml/¼ pint/⅔ cup vegetable or lamb stock
4–5 waxy potatoes, peeled and thickly sliced
salt and freshly ground black pepper
1 bay leaf
2 fresh thyme sprigs
1 tbsp melted butter
2 tbsp freshly chopped herbs, to garnish
freshly cooked green beans, to serve

Preheat the oven to 170°C/325°F/Gas Mark 3. Trim any excess fat from the lamb cutlets. Heat the oil in a frying pan and brown the cutlets in batches for 3–4 minutes. Remove with a slotted spoon and reserve.

Add the onions to the frying pan and cook for 6–8 minutes until softened and just beginning to colour; remove and reserve. Stir in the flour and cook for a few seconds, then gradually pour in the stock, stirring well, and bring to the boil. Remove from the heat.

Spread the base of a large casserole dish with half the potato slices. Top with half the onions and season well with salt and pepper. Arrange the browned meat in a layer. Season again and add the remaining onions, the bay leaf and thyme. Pour in the remaining liquid from the onions and top with the remaining potatoes so that they overlap in a single layer. Brush the potatoes with the melted butter and season again.

Cover the dish and cook in the preheated oven for 2 hours, uncovering for the last 30 minutes to allow the potatoes to brown. Garnish with chopped herbs and serve immediately with green beans.

Grandma's Tips for Smoother Skin ✑

Add a little baking powder to your washing-up water, and moisturize your hands whilst you work.

Mix a little vegetable oil (sunflower, almond, olive) with granulated sugar and rub vigorously over rough skin on hands and feet (and elbows) for a few minutes. Rinse off and let your hands and feet 'air dry'.

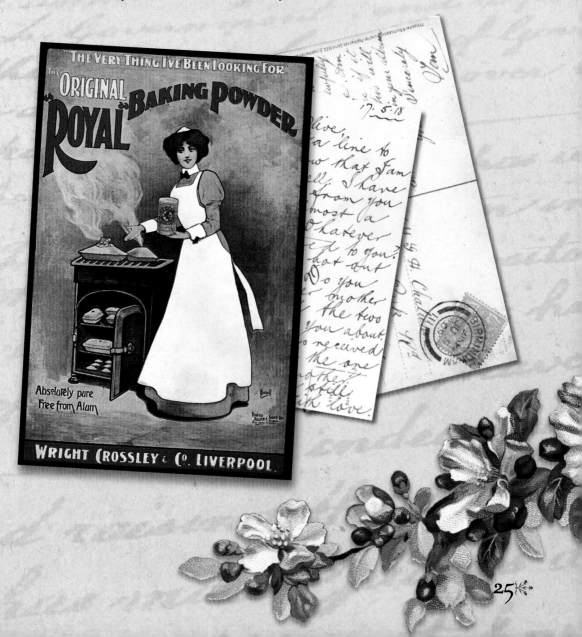

Three Bean Tagine ❦

Serves 4

Ingredients

few saffron strands
2–3 tbsp olive oil
1 small aubergine/eggplant, trimmed and diced
1 onion, peeled and chopped
350 g/12 oz/2⅔ cups peeled and diced sweet potatoes
3 medium carrots, peeled and chopped
1 cinnamon stick, bruised
1½ tsp ground cumin
salt and freshly ground black pepper
600 ml/1 pint/2½ cups vegetable stock
2 fresh mint sprigs
200 g/7 oz canned red kidney beans, drained
300 g/10 oz canned haricot beans, drained
300 g/10 oz canned flageolet beans, drained
100 g/3½ oz/¾ cup chopped ready-to-eat dried apricots
1 tbsp freshly chopped mint, to garnish

Place warm water in a small bowl and sprinkle with saffron strands. Leave to infuse for at least 10 minutes.

Heat the oil in a large heavy-based saucepan, add the aubergine/eggplant and onion and fry for 5 minutes before adding the sweet potatoes, carrots, cinnamon stick and ground cumin. Cook, stirring, until the vegetables are lightly coated in the cumin. Add the saffron with the soaking liquid and season to taste with salt and pepper. Pour in the stock and add the mint sprigs.

Rinse the beans, add to the pan and bring to the boil. Reduce the heat, cover with a lid and simmer for 20 minutes. Add the apricots and cook, stirring occasionally, for a further 10 minutes, or until the vegetables are tender. Adjust the seasoning to taste, then serve sprinkled with chopped mint.

Chicken Pie with Sweet Potato Topping ∽

Serves 4

250 g/9 oz/1⅛ cups potatoes, peeled and cut into chunks
700 g/1½ lb/4 cups sweet potatoes, peeled and cut
   into chunks
150 ml/¼ pint/⅔ cup milk
25 g/1 oz/2 tbsp butter
2 tsp brown sugar
grated zest of 1 orange
salt and freshly ground black pepper
4 skinless chicken breast fillets, diced
1 medium onion, peeled and coarsely chopped
125 g/4 oz/¼ lb baby mushrooms, stems trimmed
2 leeks, trimmed and thickly sliced
150 ml/¼ pint/⅔ cup dry white wine
1 chicken stock cube
1 tbsp freshly chopped parsley
50 ml/2 fl oz/¼ cup crème fraîche or thick double/heavy cream
green vegetables, to serve

Preheat the oven to 190°C/375°F/Gas Mark 5, 10 minutes before required. Cook the potatoes and sweet potatoes in lightly salted boiling water until tender. Drain well, return to the saucepan and mash until smooth and creamy, gradually adding the milk, then the butter, sugar and orange zest. Season to taste with salt and pepper and reserve.

Place the chicken in a saucepan with the onion, mushrooms, leeks, wine and stock cube and season to taste. Simmer, covered, until the chicken and vegetables are tender. Transfer the chicken and vegetables to a 1.1 litre/2 pint pie dish. Add the parsley and crème fraîche or cream to the liquid in the pan and bring to the boil. Simmer until thickened and smooth, stirring constantly. Pour over the chicken in the pie dish, mix and cool.

Spread the mashed potato over the chicken filling, and swirl the surface into decorative peaks. Bake in the oven for 35 minutes, or until the top is golden and the chicken filling is heated through. Serve immediately with fresh green vegetables.

Face Masks ✺

Face masks are easy to make, and can be made right here in your kitchen.

Strawberries are astringent and will close pores and tighten the skin. Just mash two or three, spread them on your face, relax for 10 minutes and rinse off.

Cherries are full of antioxidants, and a cherry and peach mixture is good for wrinkles and lines.

A yogurt and pear mix is nourishing to the skin, or use up an overripe avocado by mashing it with a squeeze of lemon and the beaten white of an egg. Let this dry on your face, then rinse off with cool water.

Sausages & Mashed Potatoes ∽

Serves 4

Ingredients

50 g/2 oz/4 tbsp butter
1 tbsp olive oil
2 large onions, peeled and thinly sliced
pinch sugar
1 tbsp freshly chopped thyme
1 tbsp plain/all-purpose flour
100 ml/3½ fl oz/⅓ cup Madeira
200 ml/7 fl oz/¾ cup vegetable stock
8–12 good-quality butchers' pork sausages,
    depending on size

For the mashed potatoes:
6–8 floury potatoes, peeled
75 g/3 oz/6 tbsp butter
4 tbsp crème fraîche/sour cream
salt and freshly ground black pepper

Melt the butter with the oil and add the onions. Cover and cook gently for about 20 minutes until the onions have collapsed. Add the sugar and stir well. Uncover and continue to cook, stirring often, until the onions are very soft and golden. Add the thyme, stir well, then add the flour, stirring. Gradually add the Madeira and the stock. Bring to the boil and simmer gently for 10 minutes.

Meanwhile, put the sausages in a large frying pan and cook over a medium heat for 15–20 minutes, turning often, until golden brown and slightly sticky all over.

For the mashed potatoes, boil the potatoes in plenty of lightly salted water for 15–18 minutes until tender. Drain well and return to the saucepan. Put the saucepan over a low heat to allow the potatoes to dry thoroughly. Remove from the heat and add the butter, crème fraîche/sour cream and salt and pepper. Mash thoroughly. Serve the mashed potatoes topped with the sausages and onion gravy.

Winter Hotchpot

Serves 4

Ingredients

small piece gammon/ham steak,
    about 300 g/11 oz
1 tbsp olive oil
1 large onion, peeled and finely chopped
2–3 garlic cloves, peeled and finely chopped
3 medium carrots, peeled and finely chopped
2 celery stalks, trimmed and finely sliced
2 leeks, trimmed and finely sliced
1 litres/2 pints/4 cups ham or vegetable stock
125 g/4 oz/⅔ cup pearl barley, rinsed
freshly ground black pepper
crusty bread, to serve

Remove any rind and fat from the gammon/ham steak and cut into small pieces.

Heat the oil in a large saucepan over a medium heat and add all the prepared vegetables and gammon. Cook, stirring occasionally, for 5–8 minutes until the vegetables have softened.

Pour in the stock and bring to the boil. Cover with a lid and simmer for 10 minutes.
Add the pearl barley to the pan.

Continue to simmer, covered, for 15–20 minutes until the vegetables and gammon are tender.
Add freshly ground black pepper to taste, then serve with crusty bread.

Household Craft: Doilies

Lace doilies make decorative coasters for drinks, desserts and vases; but you can also craft them into other attractive items for around the house. Try searching flea markets for some pretty lace doilies.

Stitch several doilies in a line to make an elegant table runner. Don't be afraid to use doilies of different sizes: a large one in the middle, working outward with smaller ones, looks very effective.

Customize a cushion cover by spreading out a prettily patterned doily over the front and sewing it on.

Pin doilies around the frame of a lampshade, and to each other. When happy with the shape, remove the doilies, stitch together, slip the cover back over the frame, and stitch to the top of the frame.

Stiffen a doily by soaking it in liquid starch, then strain it through your hand to remove excess liquid. Position it over an upturned bowl covered in plastic wrap. Leave it to dry for at least a day, then carefully remove, turn over and use your little basket.

Beef Bourgignon

Serves 4

Ingredients

700 g/1½ lb braising steak, trimmed
225 g/8 oz piece pork belly or lardons
2 tbsp olive oil
12 shallots, peeled
3 medium carrots, peeled and sliced
2 garlic cloves, peeled and sliced
2 tbsp plain/all-purpose flour
3 tbsp brandy (optional)
150 ml/¼ pint/⅔ cup red wine, such as a Burgundy
450 ml/¾ pint/1¼ cups beef stock
1 bay leaf
salt and freshly ground black pepper
450 g/1 lb new potatoes, scrubbed
1 tbsp freshly chopped parsley, to garnish

Preheat the oven to 160°C/325°F/Gas Mark 3. Cut the steak and pork into small pieces and reserve. Heat 1 tablespoon of the oil in an ovenproof casserole dish, add the meat and cook in batches for 5–8 minutes until sealed. Remove with a slotted spoon and reserve.

Add the remaining oil to the casserole dish, then add the shallots, carrots and garlic and cook for 10 minutes. Return the meat to the casserole dish and sprinkle in the flour. Cook for 2 minutes, stirring occasionally, before pouring in the brandy, if using. Heat for 1 minute, then take off the heat and ignite.

When the flames have subsided, pour in the wine and stock. Return to the heat and bring to the boil, stirring constantly. Add the bay leaf and season to taste with salt and pepper. Cover with a lid and cook in the oven for 1 hour.

Cut the potatoes in half. Remove the casserole dish from the oven and add the potatoes. Cook for a further 1 hour, or until the meat and potatoes are tender. Serve sprinkled with chopped parsley.

Fresh Strawberry Sponge Cake ∞

Serves 8–10

Ingredients

175 g/6 oz/¾ cup (1½ sticks) unsalted
   butter, softened
175 g/6 oz caster/superfine sugar
1 tsp vanilla extract
3 large/extra-large eggs, beaten
175 g/6 oz/1⅓ cups self-raising flour
150 ml/¼ pint double/heavy cream
2 tbsp icing/confectioners' sugar, sifted
225 g/8 oz (18–20 medium) fresh
   strawberries, hulled and chopped
few extra strawberries, to decorate

Preheat the oven to 190°C/375°F/Gas Mark 5, 10 minutes before baking. Lightly oil and line the bases of two 20.5 cm/8 inch round cake tins/pans with greaseproof/wax paper or baking parchment.

Using an electric mixer, beat the butter, sugar and vanilla extract until pale and fluffy. Gradually beat in the eggs a little at a time, beating well after each addition. Sift half the flour over the mixture and, using a metal spoon or rubber spatula, gently fold into the mixture. Sift over the remaining flour and fold in until just blended.

Divide the mixture between the tins, spreading evenly. Gently smooth the surfaces with the back of a spoon. Bake in the centre of the oven for 20–25 minutes until well risen and golden. Remove, leave to cool, then turn out onto a wire rack. Whip the cream with 1 tablespoon of the icing/confectioners' sugar until it forms soft peaks. Fold in the chopped strawberries.

Spread one cake layer evenly with the mixture and top with the second cake layer, rounded side up. Thickly dust the cake with icing sugar and decorate with the reserved strawberries. Carefully slide onto a serving plate and serve.

Grandma's Tip

Adding a dash of balsamic vinegar
to a recipe involving strawberries
will enhance the flavour.

Useful Cooking Solutions

Gravy too thin? Add flakes of potato or some flour.
Too salty? Add sugar or a slice of raw potato (which you can remove later).
Savoury dish too sweet? Mix in some vinegar or olive oil.
Too spicy? Add some plain yogurt or ketchup.
One egg short? If baking a cake whose ingredients include a
raising agent or self-raising flour, use 1 tablespoon vinegar instead.
Milk about to turn? Rescue it with a pinch of baking powder.
Egg shell fallen into mixture? Use another piece of shell to scoop it out.

Rich Double-Crust Plum Pie

Serves 6

Ingredients

For the pastry:
75 g/3 oz/6 tbsp butter
75 g/3 oz/6 tbsp white vegetable
 fat/shortening
225 g/8 oz/2 cups plain/all-purpose flour
2 medium/large egg yolks

For the filling:
450 g/1 lb (about 7) fresh plums,
 preferably Victoria
50 g/2 oz/4 tbsp caster/superfine sugar,
 plus a little extra
1 tbsp milk

Preheat the oven to 200°C/400°F/Gas Mark 6. Make the pastry by rubbing the butter and white vegetable fat/shortening into the flour until it resembles fine breadcrumbs, or blend in a food processor. Add the egg yolks and enough water to make a soft dough. Knead lightly, then wrap and leave in the refrigerator for about 30 minutes.

Meanwhile, prepare the fruit. Rinse and dry the plums, then cut in half and remove the stones/pits. Slice the plums into chunks and cook in a saucepan with 25 g/1 oz/2 tablespoons of the sugar and 2 tablespoons water for 5–7 minutes until slightly softened. Remove from the heat and add the remaining sugar to taste and allow to cool.

Roll out half the chilled pastry on a lightly floured surface and use to line the base and sides of a 1.1 litre/2 pint/1 quart pie dish. Allow the pastry to hang over the edge of the dish. Spoon in the prepared plums.

Roll out the remaining pastry to use as the lid and brush the edge with a little water. Wrap the pastry around the rolling pin and place over the plums.

Press the edges together to seal and mark a decorative edge around the rim of the pastry by pinching with the thumb and forefinger or using the back of a fork.

Brush the lid with milk, and make a few slits in the top. Use any trimmings to decorate the top of the pie with pastry leaves. Place on a baking sheet and bake in the oven for 30 minutes, or until golden brown. Sprinkle with a little caster/superfine sugar and serve hot or cold.

Grandma's Tip

**You can make your own caster/superfine sugar
by grinding up regular granulated sugar in a
food processor at high speed for a few seconds.**

Banana & Honey Tea Bread

Makes one 900 g/2 lb loaf

Ingredients

2 large peeled bananas, about 225 g/8 oz
1 tbsp fresh orange juice
125 g/4 oz/½ cup (8 tbsp) soft margarine
125 g/4 oz/heaping ½ cup (packed) soft light
   brown sugar
125 g/4 oz/½ cup honey
2 medium/large eggs, beaten
225 g/8 oz/heaping 1¾ cups wholemeal/
   whole-grain self-raising flour
½ tsp ground cinnamon
75 g/3 oz sultanas/golden raisins

Preheat the oven to 180°C/350°F/Gas Mark 4. Grease a 900 g/2 lb/9 x 5 x 3-inch loaf tin/pan and line the base with a strip of nonstick baking parchment. Mash the bananas together in a large bowl with the orange juice.

Place the soft margarine, sugar and honey in the bowl and add the eggs. Sift in the flour and cinnamon, adding any bran left behind in the sieve. Beat everything together until light and fluffy and then fold in the sultanas/golden raisins.

Spoon the mixture into the prepared tin and smooth the top to make it level. Bake for about 1 hour until golden, well risen and a skewer inserted into the centre comes out clean.

Cool in the tin for 5 minutes, then turn out on a wire rack.

Gingerbread

Cuts into 8 slices

Ingredients

175 g/6 oz/¾ cup (1½ sticks) butter
  or margarine
225 g/8 oz/⅔ cup black treacle/molasses
50 g/2 oz/¼ cup dark muscovado/dark
  brown sugar
350 g/12 oz/3 cups plain/all-purpose flour
2 tsp ground ginger
150 ml/¼ pint/⅔ cup milk, warmed
2 medium/large eggs
1 tsp bicarbonate of soda/baking soda
1 piece stem/preserved ginger in syrup
1 tbsp stem/preserved-ginger syrup

Preheat the oven to 150°C/300°F/Gas Mark 2, 10 minutes before baking. Lightly oil and line the base of a 20.5 cm/8 inch deep round cake tin/pan with greaseproof/wax paper or baking parchment.

In a saucepan, gently heat the butter or margarine, black treacle/molasses and sugar, stirring occasionally, until the butter melts. Leave to cool slightly. Sift the flour and ground ginger into a large bowl. Make a well in the centre, then pour in the treacle mixture. Reserve 1 tablespoon of the milk, then pour the rest into the treacle mixture. Stir together lightly until mixed.

Beat the eggs together, then stir into the mixture. Dissolve the bicarbonate of soda/baking soda in the remaining 1 tablespoon of warmed milk and add to the mixture. Beat the mixture until well combined and free of lumps. Pour into the tin and bake in the oven for 1 hour, or until well risen and a skewer inserted into the centre comes out clean. Cool in the tin, then remove. Slice the stem ginger into thin slivers and sprinkle over the cake. Drizzle with the syrup and serve.

Going to See Grandmamma (extract)

Little Molly and Damon
Are walking so far,
For they're going to see
Their kind Grandmamma.

And they very well know,
When they get there she'll take
From out of her cupboard
Some very nice cake.

by Kate Greenaway
(1846–1901)

The Flower Race.

Apple Pie

Ingredients
175 g/6 oz/heaping 1⅓ cups plain/all-purpose flour
pinch salt
40 g/1½ oz/3 tbsp lard or white vegetable fat
40 g/1½ oz/3 tbsp butter or block margarine
1 tbsp caster/superfine sugar

For the filling:
500 g/1¼ lb/4½ cups peeled,
   cored and sliced cooking apples
125 g/4 oz/⅔ cup caster/superfine sugar
1 tsp ground cinnamon
⅓ tsp ground nutmeg
50 g/2 oz/⅓ cup sultanas/golden raisins
15 g/½ oz/1 tbsp butter
milk, for glazing
caster/superfine sugar, for sprinkling

Sift the flour and salt into a bowl or a food processor and add the fats, cut into small pieces. Rub in with your fingertips, or process, until the mixture resembles fine crumbs. Mix in the sugar and add 2–3 tablespoons cold water to form a soft dough, then knead lightly until smooth. Wrap and chill for 30 minutes.

Preheat the oven to 220°C/425°F/Gas Mark 7 and grease a 1.5 litre/2½ pint/1½ quart deep pie dish/pan. Roll out the pastry on a lightly floured surface. Turn the pie dish upside down onto the pastry and cut round it to form the lid. Roll the trimmings into a 2.5 cm/1 inch strip and press this firmly onto the top edge of the dish.

Mix the sliced apples with the sugar, spices and sultanas/golden raisins. Place in the dish and then dot with butter. Dampen the pastry edge with water, then place the pastry lid over. Press the edges to seal, and flute together with your thumb and forefinger. Make a hole in the centre to allow the steam to escape, then decorate with pastry trimmings.

Brush with milk, then sprinkle with caster/superfine sugar.
Bake for 10 minutes, then turn the oven temperature down to
190°C/375°F/Gas Mark 5 and bake for a further 25–30 minutes until
crisp and golden. Serve hot straight away with cream or custard.

(Apple Pie) Air Freshener

Fill a small bowl almost to the top (choose a pretty one for added
effect) with bicarbonate of soda/baking soda and add a few drops of
your favourite essential oil. Add more oil when the effect starts to
wane and replace the whole lot every three months.

For an apple-pie spice scent, try using cinnamon and clove essential
oils, using double the amount of cinnamon to cloves.

Chocolate Orange Cookies

Makes 30

Ingredients

100 g/3½ oz dark/semisweet dark chocolate
125 g/4 oz/½ cup (1 stick) butter
125 g/4 oz/⅔ cup caster/superfine sugar
pinch salt
1 medium/large egg, beaten
grated zest of 2 oranges
200 g/7 oz/1½ cups plain/all-purpose flour
1 tsp baking powder
125 g/4 oz/1 cup icing/confectioners' sugar
1–2 tbsp orange juice

Preheat the oven to 200°C/400°F/Gas Mark 6, 15 minutes before baking. Lightly oil several baking sheets. Coarsely grate the chocolate and reserve. Beat the butter and sugar together until creamy. Add the salt, beaten egg and half the orange zest and beat again.

Sift the flour and baking powder, add to the bowl with the grated chocolate and beat to form a dough. Shape into a ball, wrap in plastic wrap and chill in the refrigerator for 2 hours.

Roll the dough out on a lightly floured surface to 5 mm/¼ inch thickness. Cut into 5 cm/2 inch rounds. Place the rounds on the prepared baking sheets, allowing room for expansion. Bake in the preheated oven for 10–12 minutes until firm. Remove the cookies from the oven and leave to cool slightly. Transfer to a wire rack and leave to cool.

Sift the icing/confectioners' sugar into a small bowl and stir in sufficient orange juice to make a smooth, spreadable icing. Spread or pipe the icing over the biscuits, leave until almost set, then sprinkle on the remaining grated orange zest before serving.

Grandma's Tip: Perfect Cookies

If your biscuits or cookies have a tendency to spread too
much when in the oven, a handy hint is to put your dough
in the refrigerator a couple of hours before baking.

Grandma's Tip: Plant Feed

After using eggs in a recipe, put the shells to good use. Make your own plant
feed by leaving broken egg shells in a watering can filled with water overnight.

Jammy Buns ∽

Makes 12

Ingredients

175 g/6 oz/heaping 1⅓ cups plain/
   all-purpose flour
175 g/6 oz/heaping 1⅓ cups wholemeal/
   whole-wheat flour
2 tsp baking powder
150 g/5 oz/⅔ cup (1¼ sticks) butter or margarine
125 g/4 oz/⅔ cup demerara/turbinado sugar
50 g/2 oz/⅓ cup dried cranberries
1 large/extra-large egg, beaten
1 tbsp milk, plus extra for brushing
4–5 tbsp seedless raspberry or strawberry jam/jelly

Preheat the oven to 190°C/375°F/Gas Mark 5, 10 minutes before baking. Lightly oil a large baking sheet. Sift the flours and baking powder together into a large bowl, then tip in the grains remaining in the sieve.

Add the butter or margarine to the flours and cut into small pieces. (It is easier to do this when the butter is in the flour, as it helps stop the butter from sticking to the knife.) Rub the butter into the flours until it resembles coarse breadcrumbs. Stir in the sugar and cranberries.

Using a round-bladed knife, stir in the beaten egg and the milk. Mix to form a firm dough. Divide the mixture into 12 and roll into balls. Place the dough balls on the baking sheet, leaving enough room for expansion.

Press your thumb into the centre of each ball to make a small hollow. Spoon a little of the jam/jelly into each hollow, and brush the top of the buns lightly with milk.
Bake in the preheated oven for 20–25 minutes until golden brown.
Cool on a wire rack and serve.

Rhubarb & Raspberry Cobbler

Serves 4

Ingredients

325 g/11½ oz/2⅔ cups rhubarb chunks
175 g/6 oz/1½ cups raspberries
50 g/2 oz/¼ cup caster/superfine sugar
1 orange

For the topping:
225 g/8 oz/1¾ cups plain/all-purpose flour
1 tbsp baking powder
50 g/2 oz/4 tbsp butter, diced
50 g/2 oz/¼ cup caster/superfine sugar
150 ml/¼ pint/scant ⅔ cup milk
custard or double/heavy cream, to serve

Preheat the oven to 220°C/425°F/Gas Mark 7. Butter a 1.7 litre/3 pint/2 quart ovenproof dish.

Mix the rhubarb chunks with the raspberries and sugar and place in the buttered dish. Finely grate the zest from the orange and set aside. Squeeze out the juice and add to the dish with the rhubarb. Cover the dish with a piece of foil and bake for 20 minutes.

For the topping, sift the flour and baking powder into a bowl and stir in the grated orange zest. Rub in the butter with your fingertips until the mixture resembles fine crumbs. Stir in the caster/superfine sugar and quickly add the milk. Mix with a fork to make a soft dough. (The mixture has to be made quickly because the leavening agent – baking powder – starts to activate as soon as liquid is added.)

Take the dish out of the oven and discard the foil. Break off rough tablespoons of the dough and drop them on top of the fruit filling. Bake for about 25 minutes until the topping is firm and golden. Serve immediately with custard or cream.

Notes on the recipes:
Please note that the measurements provided in this book are presented as 'metric/imperial/US-cups'
practical equivalents; certain food and cooking items that are termed differently in the UK
and in the US/North America are presented as 'UK term/US term'; and eggs are
medium (UK)/large (US) and large (UK)/extra-large (US).

Publisher's Note:
Raw or semicooked eggs should not be consumed by babies, toddlers,
pregnant or breast-feeding women, the elderly or people with a chronic illness.

Publisher & Creative Director: Nick Wells
Senior Project Editor: Catherine Taylor
Publishing Assistant: Laura Bulbeck
Art Director: Mike Spender
Layout Design: Jane Ashley
Digital Design & Production: Chris Herbert

Special thanks to Digby Smith and Helen Wall.

First published 2011 by
FLAME TREE PUBLISHING
Crabtree Hall, Crabtree Lane
Fulham, London SW6 6TY
United Kingdom
www.flametreepublishing.com

Flame Tree is part of The Foundry Creative Media Company Limited

Picture Credits
All images courtesy of Foundry Arts except for the following, which are © Fine Art Photographic Library:
4, 26c George Smith (1829–1901), *Here's Granny*, 1876; 5 Joseph Clark (1834–1926), *A Family Gathering*; 7b Joseph Moseley Barber
(fl.1858–89), *A Farmhouse Kitchen*; 9cr Paul Gagneux (d. 1892), *A Still Life Of Plums And Jam-Making Utensils*; 16c Joseph Clark
(1834–1926), *Playing With The Kitten*; 17t William Kay Blacklock (1872–1924), *By the Fireside*; 20 Charles Green (1804–98),
Christmas Comes but Once a Year!; 23 Mary Evelina Kindon (fl. 1879–1918), *Saying Grace*; 25 artist unknown, *Poster: Royal Baking
Powder*, c. 1900; 29 Frederick Morgan (1856–1927), *Cherry Earrings*; 32t Charles Hunt (1803–1877), *Minding the Baby*; 35 artist
unknown, *A Lesson In Cookery*, from 'Chatterbox', 1906; 38 artist unknown, *Grannie's Portrait*; 45 Norman Prescott-Davies
(1862–1915), *A Dry Summer*, 1891
and courtesy of Shutterstock:
Recurring lace border: © Karolina L; 7t, 13cl, 31b © bioraven; 8b, 13t, 14c, 15c, 16tl, 17b, 19cl, 21c, 30tr,
33bl, 41tl © Canicula; 9t © Khomulo Anna; 9cl © mart; 10tr © JaneH; 10bl © Robyn Mackenzie; 13bl
© Smit; 16tr, 44tr © nito; 18, 40 © dionisvera; 26br, 38br; 28br, 37t, 37b, 39b, 44b, 46tr

Printed in China